The Ten Plagues

The story of the children of Israel and Pharaoh

Exodus 7–12 for children

Written by Sara Hartman

Illustrated by Terri Murphy

Arch® Books
Copyright © 2006 Concordia Publishing House
3558 S. Jefferson Avenue, St. Louis, MO 63118-3968
1-800-325-3040 • www.cph.org

Manufactured in Colombia

Moses told Pharaoh, ruler of Egypt,
"God wants my people to go
To worship Him in the desert."
But Pharaoh told Moses, "No!"

The Israelites were Pharaoh's slaves;
They worked hard every day
To build great cities in Egypt.
Pharaoh wanted to keep it that way.

But he needed to learn the lesson
That God was in command.
God decided to send troubles,
Called plagues, across the land.

Because they were His people,
God protected each Israelite
From the plagues that He would send
To show Egypt His power and might.

God told Aaron, the brother of Moses,
To hold his staff over the Nile.
God turned all the water to blood,
Fish died, and the smell was vile.

Then Moses again told Pharaoh,
"You *must* let us do as God asks."
But Pharaoh's heart was hard as stone,
And he kept them doing their tasks.

God sent frogs to bug the Egyptians:
Frogs in houses, in food, in the streets.
The people found frogs everywhere,
In their clothes and under their sheets.

"Get rid of the frogs!" begged Pharaoh,
"And I will let your people go pray."
But when God took away the plague,
Pharaoh once again said, "No way!"

God sent gnats to bite the Egyptians.
Moses said, "Let my people go!"
But Pharaoh's heart remained hardened,
And again he told Moses, "No!"

God sent flies to pester Egypt.
Pharaoh said the slaves could depart,
But once the plague was lifted,
Pharaoh had a change of heart.

So God sent a plague on the livestock.
All the animals died in the field,
Except those owned by Israelites.
Still Pharaoh would not yield.

Next Moses threw ash in the air.
When it fell on an Egyptian's skin,
It turned into painful sores.
Still Pharaoh's will did not bend.

Moses said, "Surely the plagues will continue
If you don't let the Israelites go.
Now bring your slaves in from the fields.
A hailstorm is coming tomorrow."

God sent thunder and lightning and hail—
The biggest storm of its kind.
Pharaoh cried, "Stop the storm; you may go!"
But then, he again changed his mind.

God sent locusts to finish the job
Of destroying Egyptian crops.
Once more Pharaoh said the slaves could go,
And once more he told them to stop.

Moses stretched out his hand toward the sky,
And darkness fell over the land.
For three days Egypt lived in darkness.
Still Pharaoh did not understand.

Then God sent the tenth and last plague
To show Pharaoh His might and power.
He killed all of Egypt's firstborn sons
At midnight's darkest hour.

But Israel's firstborn were spared
If lamb's blood was spread on the door.
It was a saving sign from God,
And the angel of death passed them o'er.

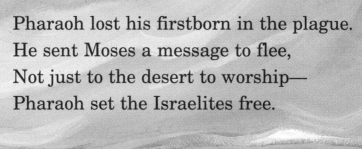

Pharaoh lost his firstborn in the plague.
He sent Moses a message to flee,
Not just to the desert to worship—
Pharaoh set the Israelites free.

God will always deliver His people
From whatever trouble we're in.
He sent Moses to help the Israelite slaves,
And Jesus to die for our sins.

Dear Parents,

"Pharaoh will not listen to you. Then I will lay My hand on Egypt and bring My hosts, My people the children of Israel, out of the land of Egypt by great acts of judgment." (Exodus 7:4)

The story of the ten plagues of Egypt helps us to remember what happens to us when we harden our hearts as Pharaoh did. Although Pharaoh asked Aaron and Moses to plead to the Lord on his behalf when things got rough, when the Lord lifted each plague, Pharaoh was back to his old ways. He refused to change. How often do we do the same? How often do we ask things of God, promising to do something in return, then don't do what we promised? This story reminds us to follow God's wishes and not our own. We should remember the devotion of Moses and how he kept doing what the Lord asked although it seemed like the Israelites would never be free as God had promised.

This story offers a great opportunity to remind your child that God keeps His promises and protects those that love Him. Tell your child that every time we are hurt, tired, or lonely that we can be comforted because we know God will watch over us just like He did the Israelites. As He promises us in His Word, God will always take care of those that love Him: "And we know that for those who love God all things work together for good, for those who are called according to His purpose" (Romans 8:28).

The Editor

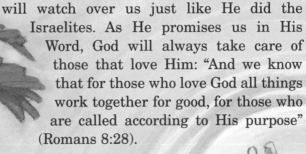